ACHIEVING JOB SATISFACTION

A Crisp Assessment Profile

The Editors of Crisp Publications, Inc.

A FIFTY-MINUTE™ SERIES BOOK

CRISP PUBLICATIONS, INC.
Menlo Park, California

ACHIEVING JOB SATISFACTION
A Crisp Assessment Profile

The Editors of Crisp Publications, Inc.

CREDITS:
Editor: **Kay Kepler**
Typesetting: **ExecuStaff**
Cover Design: **Carol Harris**
Artwork: **Ralph Mapson**

English language Crisp books are distributed worldwide. Our major international distributors include:

CANADA: Reid Publishing, Ltd., Box 69559—109 Thomas St., Oakville, Ontario Canada L6J 7R4. TEL: (416) 842-4428, FAX: (416) 842-9327

AUSTRALIA: Career Builders, P.O. Box 1051, Springwood, Brisbane, Queensland, Australia 4127. TEL: 841-1061, FAX: 841-1580

NEW ZEALAND: Career Builders, P.O. Box 571, Manurewa, Auckland, New Zealand. TEL: 266-5276, FAX: 266-4152

JAPAN: Phoenix Associates Co., Mizuho Bldg. 2-12-2, Kami Osaki, Shinagawa-Ku, Tokyo 141, Japan. TEL: 3-443-7231, FAX: 3-443-7640

Selected Crisp titles are also available in other languages. Contact International Rights Manager Suzanne Kelly at (415) 323-6100 for more information.

Library of Congress Catalog Card Number 93-79281
The Editors, Crisp Publications, Inc.
Achieving Job Satisfaction
ISBN 1-56052-257-7

This book is printed on recyclable paper with soy ink.
PRINTED WITH SOY INK

ABOUT THIS BOOK

Achieving Job Satisfaction is not like most books. It has a unique "self-paced" format that encourages a reader to become personally involved. Designed to be "read with a pencil," there is an abundance of exercises, activities, assessments and cases that invite participation.

This book is for anyone who has wondered if there is more to a job than just work. Each reader can survey his or her attitudes about the ten sources of job satisfaction. Each source is explored in depth, with fun and creative solutions presented to help readers improve their job satisfaction in all areas.

Achieving Job Satisfaction (and the other self-improvement books listed in the back of this book) can be used effectively in a number of ways. Here are some possibilities:

—**Individual Study.** Because the book is self-instructional, all that is needed is a quiet place, some time and a pencil. By completing the activities and exercises, a reader should not only receive valuable feedback, but also practical steps in creating a more meaningful work experience.

—**Workshops and Seminars.** The book is ideal for reading prior to a workshop or seminar. With the basics in hand, the quality of participation will improve. More time can be spent on concept extensions and applications during the program. The book is also effective when a trainer distributes it at the beginning of a session and leads participants through the contents.

—**Remote Location Training.** Copies can be sent to those not able to attend "home office" training sessions.

—**Informal Study Groups.** Thanks to the format, brevity and low cost, this book is ideal for "brown-bag" or other information group sessions.

There are other possibilities that depend on the objectives, program or ideas of the user. One thing is certain; even after it has been read, this book will serve as excellent reference material that can be easily reviewed.

PREFACE

Do you sometimes wonder why your work is not more satisfying? Is it becoming increasingly difficult to generate enthusiasm for your job? Do you see more problems with your job than you ever have before? If so, do you want to do something about it?

To take a more positive view of the work you do—no matter what it may be—you need look no further than your personal level of job satisfaction. It's that simple. Just determine the true sources of your job satisfaction and, with a few adjustments, you will discover that you can make work more pleasurable. As a consequence, your productivity will increase and your career will benefit. Are you willing to give it a try?

Read on . . .

CONTENTS

P A R T

I

Accepting the
Challenge

WHAT IS JOB SATISFACTION?

Job satisfaction is the fulfillment and gratification that comes from work. It is not the money, the benefits or the vacations. It is the good feelings you receive from doing the work itself. Virtually every job can provide a level of satisfaction:

- A supervisor who successfully performs the role as a team leader each day probably drives home after work with a feeling of satisfaction.

- A technician who discovers and repairs a device that has stalled production probably takes pride in the accomplishment.

- A teacher who recognizes students' achievements probably derives satisfaction from their progress.

Job satisfaction comes when one accepts a job for what it is and exploits the sources of satisfaction that come with it. Many different sources of satisfaction are tied to the same job. Good feelings can come from high performance, quality work, learning new skills, working as part of a team, assisting coworkers, demonstrating personal growth and receiving compliments. All workers can exploit at least 10 sources of satisfaction.

Job satisfaction is achieved daily by digging out "satisfiers" wherever they can be found. This is true even if an individual is marking time until he or she gets into a better career area. The trick is to enjoy your present job while you prepare for a better one. Many people gain considerable satisfaction from doing ordinary jobs. They make quality time out of their working hours no matter what their assignments may be.

CHANGING THE WAY YOU VIEW WORK

Let's face it! Most people do not receive as much satisfaction from their jobs as they could if they had a more positive attitude toward what they are doing.

What can be done about it?

IT'S EASY!
Instead of viewing work as something to be endured, we need to view it as a primary source of satisfaction and happiness—and work to make it happen.

This means digging deeply within ourselves and changing our focus on the work that we do. Why are such changes so difficult? Probably for these reasons:

- We have trained ourselves to avoid work instead of to enjoy it. Work is something we must do to live; it is not a source of personal fulfillment. Unless we can change this attitude, job satisfaction is out of reach.

- We close our eyes to the fact that our job can provide satisfactions that can be found no place else.

- We assume that management provides most of what we like best about our jobs when, in truth, most satisfactions come only through our own efforts.

Management, of course, should do everything possible to provide and encourage job satisfaction, but learning to view work in a more positive way is a highly personal challenge. To be successful, the effort must come from within. Employees must acknowledge that management cannot slip a certificate of job satisfaction in a paycheck envelope.

LOOK TO YOURSELF

The basic equation of employment is fairly simple. Under normal circumstances management expects certain contributions from employees (productivity, dependability, cooperation, etc.) and employees anticipate certain rewards from management (good pay, benefits, quality supervision, etc.). When the contributions and rewards are somewhat balanced, work becomes a win-win situation.

Under this mutual reward system, it is only natural that employees look to management for job satisfaction along with the other rewards. But the truth is that many primary sources of job satisfaction are accessible only to each individual employee.

Sources of satisfaction come from two areas.

1. First is the satisfaction of doing a job right—the pride of craft—regardless of the work environment. A cabinet maker gets pleasure from building a quality cabinet no matter where the cabinet is built or with whom. A surgeon gets satisfaction from performing a difficult operation whether the operating theater is in a highly rated hospital or an army tent. Computer operators, secretaries and dishwashers can get satisfaction from doing the job right. Of course, it is more difficult to find satisfaction in some jobs than in others, especially when you recognize that you are temporarily underemployed but need the job anyway.

2. The second area in which to find job satisfaction is the work environment, which includes the physical setup, people with whom you interact and the fun you can have when you are not concentrating on the work. You might be on the cleanup crew for a movie producer. The job itself may provide little satisfaction, but being around movie people in different locations might provide many satisfactions.

Between the two—performing your job skills and your work environment—you have 10 primary sources of satisfaction. To enjoy maximum benefits from these sources, you must forget about the satisfactions you might receive from a different, more appropriate job or additional things your supervisor might do for you to help. Your challenge is simply to get more satisfaction from your present job—the way it exists now.

HOW TO TELL WHEN WORKERS ARE GETTING JOB SATISFACTION

Observe workers as they arrive for work and depart for home. Those who feel job satisfaction usually reflect that in the way they walk, dress and greet others. They seem enthusiastic. It won't take 30 minutes and two cups of coffee to get them started. These workers are ready when they arrive.

The same employees have a feeling of accomplishment at the end of the day that is reflected in their upbeat conversations with others. They are ready to get into leisure because they know they have earned it.

Employees with low job satisfaction levels arrive for work without much anticipation. They move slowly and refuse responsibility for making it a good work day. They are disinterested, unenthusiastic, and carry an attitude that defies others who might try to lighten their burden.

The same employees may appear joyful at the end of the work day, not because they have had a satisfying day, but because it is over. Their joy, however, is shallow when compared to workers who experience eight hours of job satisfaction.

Do you know of a place where you might observe this phenomenon? Not where you work, but somewhere else where you could be objective? If so, give it a try. The experience may not reveal the inner ingredients of job satisfaction, but the outer manifestations could prove revealing.

I would describe my attitude at work as _____

_____

What I like best about my job is _____

_____

To get myself out of an attitude slump I _____

_____

Why High Job Satisfaction Leads to Career Success

Do supervisors and employees who squeeze more satisfaction out of their jobs enjoy greater career success? Are they promoted ahead of others? Do they earn better assignments for themselves? Do they make more money?

For years, career counselors have been saying, "If you can find a job that gives satisfaction, you will automatically be more successful and make more money."

As simple as that statement may be, it remains true today. Why is this true?

- When you are satisfied, you release your inner enthusiasm and creativity.

- When you are happy, you are more positive, which keeps those around you more positive.

- Having job satisfaction usually pleases management—so when you please yourself you also please your boss.

- With high job satisfaction you build better relationships with superiors, coworkers and customers because satisfaction is infectious.

- When things are going well on the job, you do not look for ways to escape work; rather, you look for more meaningful assignments.

- When you are satisfied, you stay more focused so you make fewer mistakes.

Many workers strategize to achieve career success. They play politics, jump through hoops and do whatever else they think will help them up the career ladder. These people often ignore the fact that job satisfaction can bring career success more easily, ethically and efficiently. When you have job satisfaction, you come closer to your potential. Your achievements help you stand out. Being excited about your job eventually draws success to you. You make the same trip up the job ladder as the plotters and the planners, but you enjoy it more.

LIVE UP TO YOUR POTENTIAL

We can do more than just show up for work and take up space; we can contribute to the organizations that employ us. We do this through our specific job and other assignments. Potential is the combination of our abilities, aptitudes, talents, stamina and attitude. We all have different potentials and, as diagrammed below, some of us have a higher potential to contribute than others.

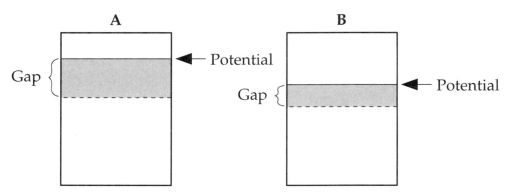

The truth is, however, that none of us ever totally lives up to our potential. There is always a gap between what we could do and our actual performance. We gain satisfaction from trying harder. A worker with a modest potential (B above) who tries to do more achieves more satisfaction than a worker with higher potential (A above) who produces more and tries less. It is the size of the gap that is important: the smaller the gap, the more job satisfaction.

Why is this true? Consider these possibilities and check any that apply to you.

☐ When I am pushing to reach my potential, I know I am in the race. I understand that I am stretching myself and this feels good.

☐ I am learning more. My mind can go stale if it does not receive new and exciting stimuli. When I am trying to achieve my potential, my mind is open and it is satisfying to receive new ideas.

☐ I am pleasing my boss and earning the respect of coworkers, which may provide me with recognition that is also satisfying.

☐ When I know I am performing near my potential, I feel good about my contribution. I am proud of my accomplishment whether anyone recognizes it or not.

Just getting by in a job does not provide much personal satisfaction. Living close to your potential is just the opposite. You leave your job each day feeling you have accomplished something important.

P A R T

II

The Psychology of
Job Satisfaction

JOB SATISFACTION SCALE

Do you ever wonder if you are getting as much satisfaction from your job as you should? Are you willing to search out the sources of satisfaction that exist? If you discover ways to enjoy your job more, might you consider making changes?

It's time to assess the personal satisfaction—sense of accomplishment, personal rewards, fulfillment, even pleasure—you get from your job. We are not talking about how much money you make, what kind of work you do, or other physical factors. We are talking exclusively about the psychological elements you control with your attitude.

To make this assessment, dig deeply within yourself and measure the satisfaction you receive from the 10 sources listed below. Afterward, you will have the information to prepare a job satisfaction profile that will help you decide if you want to make changes to increase your job satisfaction.

After you have complted the *Job Satisfaction Scale* that follows you should have greater insight into ten primary sources of job satisfaction. Please keep in mind that gaining additional job satisfaction is primarily up to you as an employee. The good news is that you are also the primary beneficiary.

Instructions

STEP 1: Starting on the next page, read each of the 10 paragraphs that define the 10 sources of job satisfaction. Relate what you read to your present responsibilities.

STEP 2: Using the scale in the right-hand margin, rate the amount of satisfaction you get from each source on a scale from 1 to 10 (10 being the highest). If you rate a source from 1 to 4, you receive little satisfaction. If you rate a source 5, 6 or 7, you receive modest gratification or fulfillment. If your satisfaction is high, a rating of 8, 9 or 10 may be appropriate. Keep in mind that a rating of 10 is unusual. Few people gain such a high degree of satisfaction from any source. On the other hand, it is normal to get a low score in one or more categories. The more honest you are with yourself, the more the finished profile will mean to you. This is your personal inventory, so there are no right or wrong answers.

STEP 3: When you have a score for each source, turn to the profile sheet and draw a point in each column indicating your level of satisfaction. Follow this procedure for all 10 categories.

STEP 4: Total your scores and write the answer in the square provided.

RATING YOUR SOURCES OF JOB SATISFACTION

Rate yourself on the scale with a checkmark.

1. *PRODUCTIVITY*

''A full day's work makes me feel good.''

Most workers gain satisfaction from turning out a good day's work. Many individuals enjoy a good feeling heading home in the evening after a competitive and productive day. If you regularly receive satisfaction from living up to your productivity potential, give this source a high rating. If you recognize that when your productivity is high you feel somewhat better than on down days, give yourself a 5 or slightly better. If you recognize the feeling but it does little for you, a lower rating would be in order.

10 ☐
9 ☐
8 ☐
7 ☐
6 ☐
5 ☐
4 ☐
3 ☐
2 ☐
1 ☐

2. *QUALITY OF WORK*

''I get my kicks from doing quality work.''

It is satisfying to be recognized by superiors and coworkers as a high producer, but it can be equally satisfying to be known as a ''quality'' producer. Workers who enjoy doing things right can be called master workers. They love to turn out quality products or services. It is not so much receiving recognition from others as it is the satisfaction from within. Do you do high quality work? Do you reach beyond normal standards of efficiency and precision on your present job?

10 ☐
9 ☐
8 ☐
7 ☐
6 ☐
5 ☐
4 ☐
3 ☐
2 ☐
1 ☐

3. *LEARNING*

''I take pride in keeping my skill level high.''

To do quality work, you need to keep learning and continually upgrade your professional skills. It takes a positive learning attitude to do this. Do you enjoy being ahead of others when it comes to advancing your skills? Do you subscribe to trade magazines or attend classes to keep up with changes? If so, you should gain extra satisfaction from being the ''knowledge expert'' where you work and feel comfortable giving yourself a high score. Keep in mind, however, that satisfaction is in the learning, not just in the knowing.

10 ☐
9 ☐
8 ☐
7 ☐
6 ☐
5 ☐
4 ☐
3 ☐
2 ☐
1 ☐

4. EXPRESSING CREATIVITY

"Being in the know pumps me up."

When you are contributing, expressing yourself and releasing your creativity, you gain satisfaction. It is the feeling that comes through empowerment. Instead of being left behind, you are doing your part to solve problems. Involvement also means the opportunity to be creative—to introduce new ideas, techniques and procedures that will increase productivity. If you are both involved and have found ways to express yourself in your present job, give yourself a high score. If you feel you are too far from the center of things and have little chance to express yourself, a lower score is indicated.

10 ☐
9 ☐
8 ☐
7 ☐
6 ☐
5 ☐
4 ☐
3 ☐
2 ☐
1 ☐

---

5. PROFESSIONALISM—A SENSE OF PRIDE

"It's cool to know you are a 'pro' at what you do."

Working, in some respects, is like playing a game. The better you play, the more pride you can have in yourself. When you perform to capacity, with few mistakes, you can take pride in a job well done. No matter what you do for a living, satisfaction can be gained by being a professional. How professional do you consider yourself?

10 ☐
9 ☐
8 ☐
7 ☐
6 ☐
5 ☐
4 ☐
3 ☐
2 ☐
1 ☐

---

6. RECOGNITION

"Praise for high performance is most satisfying."

Recognition is the psychic reward for doing an excellent job. Many dedicated and productive workers leave their jobs when they do not receive the recognition they feel they have earned. To some, recognition is a primary source of satisfaction and can be more important than monetary rewards. Recognition comes from many sources, including management, coworkers, customers and friends. Do people recognize your accomplishments? If you are earning all possible praise, give yourself a 9 or 10. If you are earning a more modest level of praise, perhaps an average score would be appropriate. If, however, you feel you have earned more recognition than you are receiving, give yourself a lower score.

10 ☐
9 ☐
8 ☐
7 ☐
6 ☐
5 ☐
4 ☐
3 ☐
2 ☐
1 ☐

RATING YOUR SOURCES OF JOB SATISFACTION (continued)

7. *TEAMWORK*

"It feels great to share in a team victory."

If you have been a member of a winning sports team, you know the great feeling of inner satisfaction that comes from being a team member. There is a sense of camaraderie, the status that comes from being accepted into a group, the knowledge that you will share in victories and defeats. Everyone who works together is a member of a team or family. The rewards from being a team member are substantial. What rewards are you receiving from your present job that can be attributed to being a contributing member of a team? If there is little or no team spirit where you work, your level of satisfaction from this source must be low. If you are a member of a work team and you gain high satisfaction from it, a high score is indicated.

10 ☐
9 ☐
8 ☐
7 ☐
6 ☐
5 ☐
4 ☐
3 ☐
2 ☐
1 ☐

---

8. *SOCIAL SATISFACTION*

"Many of my best friends are co-workers."

Working relationships can become very satisfying. You often hear people say: "Some of my best friends are coworkers and customers." We develop mutual respect for each other and although we rarely communicate away from work, our relationship is significant to both parties. Many workers are anxious to return to work toward the end of a vacation, not because they miss their work, but because they miss their coworkers or friends. Do your work contacts fulfill much of your need to be with people? Would you be lonely without them? How much of your job satisfaction comes from social contacts at work? If this is a source of considerable personal satisfaction for you, a high rating is indicated.

10 ☐
9 ☐
8 ☐
7 ☐
6 ☐
5 ☐
4 ☐
3 ☐
2 ☐
1 ☐

9. *PERSONAL GROWTH*

We sometimes sense a feeling of deep satisfaction when we experience a degree of new personal growth. Examples might be receiving accolades from a staff presentation you worried about; acting, for the first time, as a mentor; or teaching a new employee a skill you had a difficult time learning yourself. Such experiences are deeply satisfying because we recognize that we have reached a new level of personal confidence and self-worth. If your job provides frequent opportunities for personal growth and you take advantage of them, a high rating is in order.

10 ☐
9 ☐
8 ☐
7 ☐
6 ☐
5 ☐
4 ☐
3 ☐
2 ☐
1 ☐

10. *WORK ENIVORNMENT REWARDS*

Two factors are involved: physical and psychological. First, a job is located in a physical environment that provides satisfaction, for example, outdoors near the beach or mountains or inside amusement parks or upscale retail stores. Second, you may work in a sup- portive climate where you know management is behind you and personal requests will be honored if at all possible, or you may have opportunities to "clown it up" a little or relax occasionally.

If both factors are present to a high degree, give yourself a 9 or 10. If only one is present, give yourself a middle score. If neither is present, a lower rating is indicated. Keep in mind, however, you are entitled to a higher score only if you appreciate and make the most of your fortunate work environment.

10 ☐
9 ☐
8 ☐
7 ☐
6 ☐
5 ☐
4 ☐
3 ☐
2 ☐
1 ☐

PROFILE SHEET

Use this sheet to plot the number-answer from each category of job satisfaction. The 10 categories listed indicate the primary sources of psychological satisfaction that can be found in most jobs.

	1	2	3	4	5	6	7	8	9	10
Productivity										
Quality of Work										
Learning										
Expressing Creativity										
Professionalism										
Recognition										
Teamwork										
Social Satisfaction										
Personal Growth										
Work Environment Rewards										

Low Satisfaction Level   High Satisfaction Level

TOTAL OF ALL SCORES ☐

INTERPRETING YOUR PROFILE

If your score was 75 or higher, congratulations! You get a lot of satisfaction from your job. If your score was between 50 and 75, you seem to be getting fulfillment from your work, but not as much as you could. A score of 50 or less is a signal that you could benefit from taking a new look at the way you work.

It is normal for you to rate yourself high in some categories, midrange in others and lower in a few. Very few individuals receive high satisfaction from all 10 sources.

One reason for low scores is that some people refuse to recognize that they can gain satisfaction from doing the kind of work management appreciates. For example, the first five sources (productivity, quality of work, learning, creativity and professionalism) are all qualities that help one succeed in a career, but they also provide inner satisfaction for most workers. Put another way, individuals who do not live up to their work potentials deny themselves certain satisfactions.

High scores from any source is a signal that a higher score in other categories is possible. One high score, however, may create a blind spot for another. For example, a competitive worker may get high personal satisfaction from maintaining a high level of productivity, but the same employee fails to see that the same high degree of satisfaction might be achieved from doing higher quality work. If quality became as important as quantity, job satisfaction would increase.

Obviously, some of the satisfaction you receive from your job comes from your boss or team leader. You can't give yourself public recognition. When you increase your job satisfaction from the first five sources, you automatically set yourself up to receive more satisfaction from those that remain. The sources of job satisfaction are interrelated. In the final analysis, the satisfaction you receive from your job depends primarily on your attitude. The more satisfaction you seek, the more you will find.

HOW DO YOU COMPARE?

COMPARING INDIVIDUAL PROFILES

To assist you in comparing your scores with others, three profiles are presented on the following pages. The interpretation at the bottom of each profile is designed to help you understand your personal profile better. It can also be helpful to compare your scores with that of a friend or coworker, especially if an open discussion follows.

Try this: Rate a close friend or coworker and have them rate you. Then match scores. It is often a surprise to discover that others' perceptions can be quite different from your own.

Profile #1: Mary J.

	1	2	3	4	5	6	7	8	9	10
Productivity									●	
Quality of Work										●
Learning								●		
Expressing Creativity					●					
Professionalism							●			
Recognition		●								
Teamwork						●				
Social Satisfaction								●		
Personal Growth							●			
Work Environment Rewards									●	

Low Satisfaction Level   High Satisfaction Level

TOTAL OF ALL SCORES 71

Interpretation

A score of 71 is very good. The only thing that kept it from being excellent was a low score in recognition. Mary J. is obviously a valuable employee who possesses high technical and human skills. The organization may be in danger of losing her services if more recognition from her superior is not forthcoming. On the other hand, her low recognition score may mean that Mary J. should be more aggressive in seeking deserved recognition. A good start would be to discuss the profile sheet with her immediate supervisor, who may have mis-interpreted Mary J.'s contribution to the organization. A discussion of the profile could improve the relationship and provide more recognition in the future, which could spark a higher degree of involvement on Mary J.'s part.

Profile #2: John L.

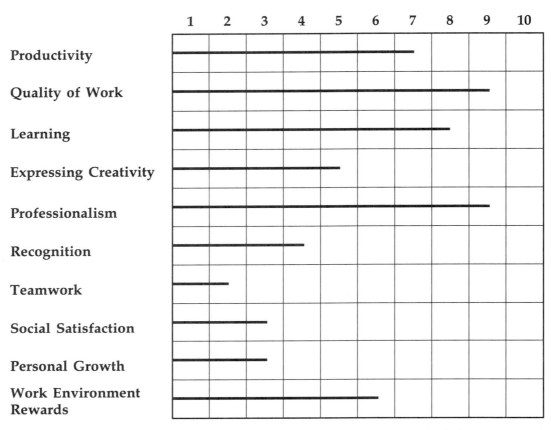

	1	2	3	4	5	6	7	8	9	10
Productivity										
Quality of Work										
Learning										
Expressing Creativity										
Professionalism										
Recognition										
Teamwork										
Social Satisfaction										
Personal Growth										
Work Environment Rewards										

Low Satisfaction Level   High Satisfaction Level

TOTAL OF ALL SCORES 53

Interpretation

John L. appears to be a strong producer with high quality. He continues to learn and views himself as a professional. It could be that John finds it difficult to mix freely with his coworkers and communicate with his boss. Making a greater effort to gain satisfaction from working more as a team member and joining in with others for a little fun and socialization might motivate John to gain more satisfaction from other sources. One gets the impression that John does not understand the connection between enjoying coworkers—being a good team member—and departmental productivity. Perhaps he likes his job but has become bored with his fellow employees. It must be difficult for John to stay upbeat when his job satisfaction from so many sources is average or below.

Profile #3: Judy R.

	1	2	3	4	5	6	7	8	9	10
Productivity										
Quality of Work										
Learning										
Expressing Creativity										
Professionalism										
Recognition										
Teamwork										
Social Satisfaction										
Personal Growth										
Work Environment Rewards										

Low Satisfaction Level   High Satisfaction Level

TOTAL OF ALL SCORES 41

Interpretation

Judy R.'s score of 41 is low and signals that she may have a negative attitude that prevents greater job satisfaction. The only score above average is *Work Environment Rewards,* which indicates Judy has a pleasant and supportive work atmosphere. Under such a climate it is hard to justify the other low scores. Judy has three options: continue to just "get by" with low job satisfaction; make a special commitment to get more satisfaction from all sources—one at a time; or start a serious search for a different job.

COMPARING INDIVIDUAL PROFILES TO NORMS

On the following pages you will find norms or averages among typical employees and supervisors. The norms in each category should be used for general comparisons only, as indications of what might be found in other employee or supervisory groups. Do not take them literally, because:

- The norms are based on a limited number of completed scales—200 for employees and less than 50 for supervisors.

- Only four work environments are represented—office, retail, medical and production.

- It is difficult for employees and supervisors to measure their own job satisfaction even with the help of the scale; thus, the norms presented should be used for conjecture and discussion purposes only.

Large organizations are encouraged to use the *Job Satisfaction Scale* to establish their own norms so that similar job situations can be compared and analyzed department by department.

EMPLOYEE JOB SATISFACTION NORMS

(Based on scores of 200 completed profiles)

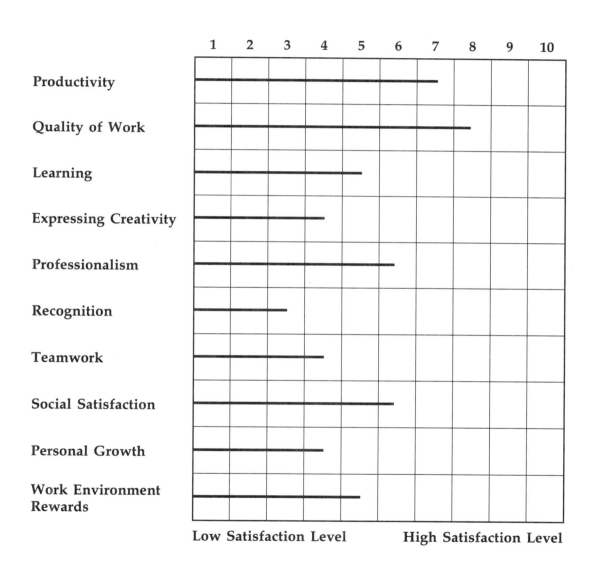

	1	2	3	4	5	6	7	8	9	10
Productivity										
Quality of Work										
Learning										
Expressing Creativity										
Professionalism										
Recognition										
Teamwork										
Social Satisfaction										
Personal Growth										
Work Environment Rewards										

Low Satisfaction Level   High Satisfaction Level

TOTAL LEVEL OF SATISFACTION THAT INCLUDES ALL 10 NORMS   52

EMPLOYEE JOB SATISFACTION NORMS (continued)

Interpretation of Employee Norms

Employees will be interested in comparing their scores against the norms for three reasons:

1. Employees can feel good when they score themselves above the norm in any of the 10 job satisfaction sources. This discovery can reinforce present satisfaction levels and may motivate the individual to get more satisfaction from that source in the future.

2. Employees can discover those sources of satisfaction that they have neglected, which can lead to a commitment to get greater satisfaction from those sources in the future.

3. The total level of satisfaction among all employees (the score in the box at the bottom of the scale) can give employees an idea of whether they are above or below average. For example, if they score themselves below 52, employees will get a signal that they need to do something to pull up their job satisfaction level. If employees score above 52, they know that they are already above average and in a better position to make further progress.

Supervisors will be interested in comparing the scores of their employees against the scores of those used to establish the norms. To do this, create a composite (average scores) of your employees to make a source-by-source comparison, which can indicate what you are doing right and where your shortcomings may lie.

A Source-By-Source Analysis of Employee Norms Raises the Following Questions:

Source	Question
Productivity	Should management be pleased with a 7 rating (average) from their employees?
Quality of Work	Might an 8 score indicate that management should set higher quality standards?
Learning	Does an average score (5) signal that supervisors should provide more learning opportunities?
Expressing Creativity	Could the score of 4 indicate that employees want to be more involved in the operations of their departments?
Professionalism	Do any employees think that they are more professional than they really are?
Recognition	Does the low score (3) say that supervisors should at least double their efforts to give employees more recognition?
Teamwork	Would this source of employee satisfaction be higher if the team concept were really working in the departments where the scale was completed?
Social Satisfaction	Does the score of 6 indicate that some employees do not desire social satisfaction from their jobs?
Personal Growth	Should the low score send a signal to supervisors to make more of an effort to provide growth opportunities for their employees?
Work Environment Rewards	Some observers believe that most employees who have excellent work environments take them for granted and, as a result, do not gain as much satisfaction as possible. Do you agree?

The editors of Crisp Publications believe that all questions probably deserve a YES answer.

COMPARING INDIVIDUAL SCORES OF SUPERVISORS AGAINST NORMS

There are three ways in which supervisors and upper management can use the norms presented on the following page.

1. The best way for supervisors to discover their effectiveness in helping employees gain job satisfaction is to compare their composite (average for each source) with established norms. A better comparison, however, would be to match scores for a similar department in their own organizations.

2. The best way to compare supervisors' level of job satisfaction is to match their scores with norms. Here again, a better comparison would be to match scores with fellow supervisors in similar jobs.

3. In addition to discovering the level of satisfaction employees have under each supervisor, management may wish to establish norms among supervisors for comparison purposes. This could help management discover if supervisors with the highest level of personal job satisfaction can transmit this to their own employees.

MANAGEMENT JOB SATISFACTION NORMS

(Based upon the scores of more than 50 profiles completed by supervisors)

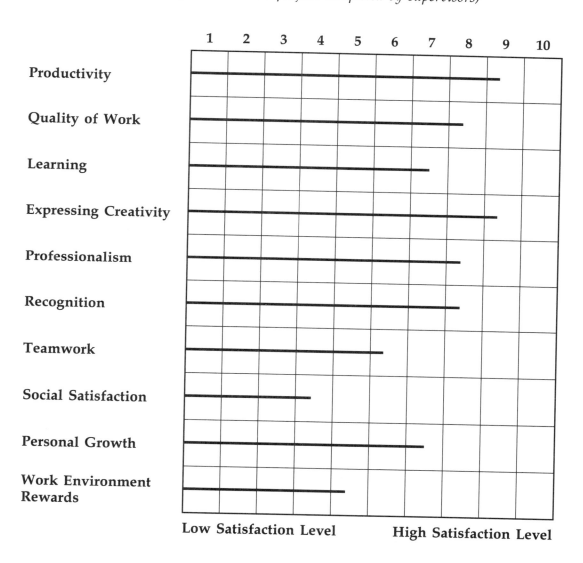

Productivity

Quality of Work

Learning

Expressing Creativity

Professionalism

Recognition

Teamwork

Social Satisfaction

Personal Growth

Work Environment Rewards

Low Satisfaction Level   High Satisfaction Level

TOTAL LEVEL OF SATISFACTION
THAT INCLUDES ALL 10 NORMS   71

(Management norms are 19 points higher than employee norms)

A Source-By-Source Analysis of Supervisory Norms Raises the Following Questions:

Source	Question
Productivity	Does such a high rating (9) indicate that most supervisors are more satisfied with their jobs than the employees they supervise? Or is it because they think they are doing a better job than they are? Or both?
Quality of Work	Did the supervisors who completed the scale rate themselves so high (8) because they were defending their performances?
Learning	Is it logical to think that supervisors rate themselves higher in this source because they have more opportunities to learn than those they supervise?
Expressing Creativity	It is natural to expect supervisors to rate themselves higher than employees in this source, but why is the gap so large? Do supervisors suppress communications among employees that they enjoy as supervisors?
Professionalism	Does supervisorial training persuade managers that they are professionals, whether it is true or not?
Recognition	Do managers gain more recognition from their superiors even though it is recognized that employees need it the most? Why do some supervisors have a blind spot when it comes to giving deserved compliments?
Teamwork	Why do management teams seem to provide more rewards than work teams?
Social Satisfaction	Is social satisfaction simply less important to managers than regular employees?
Personal Growth	If supervisors think that they experience considerable personal growth (score of 7), why can't they provide more for their employees (score of 4)?
Work Environment Rewards	Is the reason why employees do not rate this source higher because supervisors don't either (both rate it a 5)?

THE JOB SATISFACTION GAP

Why is there such a large job satisfaction gap between employees and supervisors? Consider these three possibilities:

1. Supervisors, knowing they are part of the management group, may need to defend their positions more than employees. Interviews indicate that some supervisors feel responsible for providing job satisfaction to their employees; thus, supervisors may score themselves higher because they feel they should act as models.

2. A comparison of average scores between employees and supervisors shows that supervisors feel deeply involved in the management process and therefore experience more personal growth, have more opportunities to express their creativity, more chances to learn, and can gain more recognition from their superiors than they provide their own people.

3. Supervisors rate their productivity and the quality of their leadership without being tied down to actual production figures. In other words, supervisors rate sources of job satisfaction for themselves from a more subjective point of view.

Crisp Publications will appreciate responses from those who use *The Job Satisfaction Scale* to meet special needs in their respective environments. Send your completed scale to Phil Gerould at Crisp Publications. Remain anonymous if you want, but please indicate if you are a supervisor or an employee and include your occupation and title.

P A R T

III

More Than
"Just a Job"

THE SOURCES OF SATISFACTION

Results from field tests using the *Job Satisfaction Scale* indicate that fewer than 10 percent of the participants rated themselves over 70 percent, almost 60 percent rated themselves between 50 percent and 70 percent and 40 percent rated themselves below 50.

What causes so many people to rate themselves so low in job satisfaction? Do they just have negative attitudes? Are too many of them bored because they are underemployed? Is management at fault? Are most jobs lacking in meaning no matter how workers try to jazz things up?

There are, of course, multiple reasons for low job satisfaction, but the overwhelming reason is the way employees view work. In short, many workers ignore the psychological sources of job satisfaction available to them.

What about you?

Now that you have completed and interpreted your *Job Satisfaction Profile*, let's explore the sources of satisfaction so you can take steps to make your job more satisfying. Naturally, you can make the most improvement from those sources where you rated yourself low on the scale. Please keep in mind, however, that even if you rated yourself high in a given source, some room for improvement may remain. That is why it is a good idea to refer to your *Job Satisfaction Profile* as you proceed.

SOURCE #1: PRODUCTIVITY

"I really like a boss or a job that keeps me challenged and busy. I feel better when the day is over."

—Dental Assistant

No two people will produce the same amount of work at the same job. Everyone's potential is different. Although potential cannot be measured, there is always a gap between what one is capable of doing and what one actually does. However, if you wish to raise your level of satisfaction from this source, you need to push a little more in the direction of your potential—not so much that you create too much pressure on yourself, but enough to bring you more satisfaction.

When it comes to productivity, job satisfaction comes from two sources: the joy that comes from competing with others even if you don't always win, and knowing that you are doing your best to meet or exceed your own standards or expectations.

Doing anything when you know you are not putting your best into it creates unhappiness.

Renee is a waitress in a retirement center where no tips are permitted. Yet Renee gains satisfaction in serving more tables than other waitresses. Why? "I just get a good feeling inside when I am living up to my best. This is true in everything I do. I guess it is a combination of pride, liking to compete and living up to my own standards that do the trick."

Steps to Greater Job Satisfaction

Check those you can be enthusiastic about.

☐ I refuse to be known as an "average" producer.

☐ I understand, honor and satisfy my competitive nature.

☐ I take pride in exceeding standards so that I deserve a high appraisal rating.

SOURCE #2: QUALITY WORK

"My firm now has incentives for those who improve quality as well as quantity."

—Credit Manager

Many employees are like artists who strive for superiority in their work. These individuals are never happy with mediocrity either in others or themselves. If you scored 6 or lower in this category, you may wish to work on raising your quality standards. It's a great way to get more job satisfaction in a hurry.

Jess got high marks for the amount of work he accomplished, but his manager noticed that customers tended to complain about the quality of his work. One day the manager called Jess into his office and asked: "If you were me, would you want an employee who excelled in the amount of work he did or the quality of work he turned out?" Jess thought for a few moments and replied: "I would want employees who did a lot of work without sacrificing quality."

After Jess responded the way his boss wanted, the two of them talked. Jess learned that through greater concentration he could produce at previous levels and improve his work quality. He soon discovered to his surprise that he was receiving more satisfaction from his work.

Steps to Greater Job Satisfaction

☐ I admit that doing sloppy work is unsatisfying.

☐ I recognize that with poorer quality work, I lose the satisfaction I gain through higher productivity.

☐ Without waiting for encouragement from management, I attach higher quality standards to every task I perform, and make quality a factor in my relationships with others.

SOURCE #3: LEARNING

"Wanting to learn is an attitude that can keep you from going stale on any kind of job."

—Retail Store Manager

The average score on source #3 (learning) is 5. This result means that approximately half of all employees are not taking full advantage of their on-the-job learning opportunities. Often an employee will tell you, "I just don't have any opportunities to learn on my job," but the truth is that the individual's mind is not open to the learning possibilities that exist.

If your job requires that you use a computer, you face the constant challenge of keeping up with the latest hardware and software. If you are in the building trades, you need to stay current with new techniques and equipment. If you are in a service position, your future depends on learning new features about what you sell and new techniques in the selling process. Almost all jobs have specialized skills attached to them. These competencies need to be maintained and improved if an employee wants to keep up.

"When my old firm started talking about downsizing, I started to seek learning opportunities. I applied for seminars both in-house and outside. I read the latest technical manuals. Most of all, I started to listen. This change in my learning attitude put me in the driver's seat a few years later when my job was eliminated. I was able to obtain a better position elsewhere because I had updated myself to compete in a more competitive marketplace."

Steps to Greater Job Satisfaction

☐ I will discuss with my boss what could be done to open up more learning opportunities for me.

☐ I can find a coworker who is more knowledgeable than me and build a tutoring relationship with this individual.

☐ I will develop a learning attitude by undertaking a selected reading program.

SOURCE #4: EXPRESSING CREATIVITY

''I have no desire to be a supervisor, but that doesn't mean I don't want to be involved in matters that are important to me and my patients.''

—Hospital Nurse

A lower-than-average score in this category usually means that an employee prefers to stay more isolated and express creativity off the job. The only problem with this attitude is that this employee gains less job satisfaction.

Although some jobs offer more opportunities to be involved in creative matters than do others, every job allows for some upward communication and other forms of expression. For example, when you submit a suggestion verbally or in writing to a superior, you are expressing your creativity and concern. Whether the suggestion is accepted or not is of less consequence than the fact that you expressed yourself and, as a result, have a feeling of satisfaction. As an isolated worker, you cannot feel the involvement that comes from ''being on the inside'' and sensing that you are part of a team headed for a better operation.

For three years Minerva was considered a reliable, conscientious worker. She liked her job but she felt isolated. Then, thanks to a new caring and friendly coworker, Minerva came out of her shell and expressed some creative ideas. Today Minerva's boss considers her a team player and has noticed an increase in her productivity. Now that she is expressing herself more, Minerva admits that her job is more satisfying. She says, ''For the first time, I feel I belong.''

Steps to Greater Job Satisfaction

☐ I accept with enthusiasm opportunities beyond my specific job duties. (For example, I volunteer to be a representative on an employee credit council, contribute to a newsletter or ideas to a suggestion box.)

☐ I can strengthen the way I express myself to superiors—demonstrate a stronger presence by volunteering to head a committee or undertake private research.

☐ I will give my creative nature more chance to be noticed during breaks or at lunch.

SOURCE #5: PROFESSIONALISM

"When you take pride in being professional, you view your work from a more satisfying perspective."

—Auditor

When you communicate a professional image to others, you will find your job more satisfying. Most people would agree with the following:

- *You take pride in knowing that you play by the rules. You must be ethical, honest, trustworthy, and fair in your behavior. When these conditions are present, you communicate a professionalism that is satisfying.*

- *To project a professional image, you must treat others with dignity regardless of their cultural background, education, age, race or sex. You give the same sensitive consideration to all coworkers, customers and superiors. Knowing you do this is satisfying.*

- *When you set yourself up as the kind of person others would come to for advice, you communicate professionalism. This kind of behavior usually gains respect, and when people respect you, you feel satisfaction.*

Being a professional in any type of job involves many things—living up to your potential, doing quality work, continuing to learn, expressing your creativity. It also means having high personal standards or values and living up to them. Those who accomplish this goal without becoming smug or self-important have a right to feel satisfied. They have earned respect because they have conducted themselves in a professional manner.

Steps to Greater Job Satisfaction

☐ I will go about my work in a more efficient, confident manner.

☐ I now dress the part. I have developed the image of a somewhat conservative business professional—stylish but in good taste.

☐ I always play by ethical rules—whether I win or not.

SOURCE #6: RECOGNITION

"My boss is a lost cause when it comes to paying compliments."

—Data Control Clerk

Of all the 10 sources of satisfaction in the *Job Satisfaction Scale,* recognition consistently receives the lowest scores from both employees and supervisors. This is a clear signal that employees do not receive anywhere near the recognition they need and deserve. Many employees must be content to get their recognition from customers or coworkers. Why is this necessary?

In some cases, the way in which employees build relationships with superiors is not conducive to generating compliments. Some employees may be too reticent to point out their achievements. Perhaps part of receiving earned recognition lies within each person. For example, if a worker can gain substantial job satisfaction from the other sources, more recognition will be forthcoming because it is difficult to ignore a truly satisfied person.

Katrina works hard at her job. Although she is less verbal than her coworkers, she is also more consistent, accurate and dependable. Does Katrina receive the recognition from her boss that she deserves? No. As a result, she performs at a level that does not give her the job satisfaction she desires from other sources. Mansoor produces at about the same level as Katrina and their formal appraisals are similar. But Mansoor receives steady praise and group recognition from his supervisor. The result? Mansoor is motivated to gain more satisfaction from other sources. Thus, although she is less verbal, Katrina deserves the same amount of recognition that Mansoor receives and her job satisfaction depends on it.

Steps to Greater Job Satisfaction

☐ I need to be more visible and verbal about my contributions.

☐ I can work more on building and maintaining good relationships with supervisors—keep them informed and make sure they know the contributions I make.

☐ If I follow these steps for several weeks and still do not receive adequate recognition, I will talk to my supervisor, and if management continues to take me for granted, initiate Plan B and take my services elsewhere.

SOURCE #7: TEAMWORK

"Everything you do is more rewarding when you are an accepted member of a team that is fortunate enough to have a skillful leader."

—Laboratory Technician

Working—or playing—in a team that competes and wins is especially satisfying. A group harmony develops when people who work closely together share a victory or achieve a common goal. The *esprit de corps* that can develop among team members is very satisfying and cannot be equalled by those who work in isolation.

Whether you are a member of an officially designated work team or not, there are many opportunities to share in team rewards. For example, you might work for a small business of only a dozen or so employees. In this case the entire staff would be a team and the owner would be the logical leader. You might work for a giant organization composed of many offices or production units. In this case, the "section" in which you work may constitute a team and the supervisor who tries to unify the department may still think of the staff as a "family" of workers.

Whatever your situation, the more you can work closely with coworkers to achieve common goals, the more satisfying your work can be. Teamwork at any level has many rewards.

Steps to Greater Job Satisfaction

☐ I'll act as a team member with those who work close to me, even if management does not especially encourage teams. I will cooperate with others and help them find recognition so that I can share their successes.

☐ I won't isolate myself to the extent that I am are called a loner. I will maintain my independence, but also participate as an enthusiastic member in any group endeavor.

☐ I can accept and enjoy any form of team recognition. I can create a reward (on-the-job celebration) for coworkers and myself when I think one is justified and management fails to act.

SOURCE #8: SOCIAL SATISFACTION

"It's the nice people I work with who make my job satisfying."

—Bank Teller

People are social animals who enjoy the company of others. Everyone needs friends and someone to talk to and social acceptance is high on the hierarchy of human needs.

Most people feel that communicating openly with others on a wide range of subjects is satisfying. Listening to and telling experiences, jokes or stories can be rewarding. This activity may be continually available where you work. Of course, on-the-job social contacts may be more important to some than to others.

For some workers, home responsibilities can be so demanding that little time is left for outside socialization with neighbors, friends or family. These people can satisfy their social needs at work. Some individuals like to be alone when the work day is over. They wish to spend their precious leisure time with a special hobby, listening to music or reading. These people can fill their social needs at work.

Steps to Greater Job Satisfaction

☐ I can build more and better relationships with superiors and coworkers. The better the relationships I have with others, the easier it will be to satisfy my social needs. I will be a comfortable person to know.

☐ I will practice the mutual reward theory. I will give as much of myself to others as they give to me.

☐ I'll have fun! I'll be an enthusiastic participant in on-the-job birthday and retirement parties. If more social activity is important to me, I will join a company-sponsored bowling league or similar activity.

☐ I won't spend all my breaks and lunch periods with just one or two people. I'll mix things up so I can enjoy and get to know more coworkers on an informal basis.

SOURCE #9: PERSONAL GROWTH

"Right now I am looking for a new job where more personal growth is possible."

—Supermarket Checker

Some jobs offer far more opportunities for personal growth than others. For example, a forklift operator in a warehouse probably finds it more difficult to experience personal growth than a newspaper reporter; a bus driver for a city transit system probably finds personal growth more difficult to achieve than a teacher in a classroom. This is why many "boxed in" employees return to school to prepare for new careers.

Still, most jobs offer at least some opportunity for personal growth. The forklift operator can study the science of warehousing by asking questions, noticing how wares are packaged, and becoming more efficient; the bus driver can analyze what makes the best driver and report the findings to management or become active in the transit union. Personal growth on or off the job is always a possibility.

Personal growth takes place when individuals have positive learning attitudes, set one reachable goal after another and take reasonable risks. As they enhance their abilities, gain more confidence and occupy positions of greater leadership, these people experience moments of satisfaction. They feel good about their career success—they often feel good about their personal growth whether it is connected with work or not.

Miguel started out as a dishwasher in a Mexican restaurant when he was still learning to speak English, and seven years later wound up as head chef for the same operation. To enjoy this degree of personal growth, Miguel had to be a hard and reliable worker, an outstanding observer, willing to ask questions and ready to take risks. In addition, he had to augment his on-the-job growth by taking adult education classes at night.

Steps to Greater Job Satisfaction

☐ I will prepare for and seek new levels of responsibility.

☐ When I feel inadequate in some area, I will make a commitment to upgrade myself and overcome the barrier.

☐ When the time is right, I will be confident, step out and take risks. If this requires leaving one work environment for another, I'll do it!

SOURCE #10: WORK ENVIRONMENT REWARDS

"I didn't appreciate my excellent working conditions until I heard what a few of my friends had to put up with. Now I am enjoying features I previously took for granted."

—Computer Programmer

Although employees have little control over the physical side of their work environments, they can and should appreciate the good factors that exist. For example, working in a fancy headquarters building or new industrial park can produce feelings of satisfaction. Of course, some work environments are not appealing, but even the worst of these can be improved with some imagination.

To most workers, the psychological environment is more important than the physical. Those who work under relaxed conditions, where high stress, high productivity periods are mitigated by fun, should appreciate their good fortune. Those who work in a climate where everyone is supportive and understanding should also have a feeling of satisfaction.

What about your work environment? Do you appreciate what you have? Do you have a good cafeteria where food is well-prepared and inexpensive? What about clean restrooms? Modern equipment? Protected parking? Air conditioning? Do you feel free to have enjoyable moments with coworkers without pressure? Or do you feel stifled and restricted?

Of course, you can't have everything. Only a few people can work in a luxury setting and even luxury might get tiresome. Not everyone can get paid for working on a cruise ship that travels to exotic places, but that, too, has more drawbacks than most of us know about.

Steps to Greater Job Satisfaction

☐ I will focus on the positive factors in my work environment, even if there are not as many as I would like.

☐ When I concentrate on appreciating the good parts of my environment, I won't have enough focus left to complain about the bad parts.

☐ My positive attitude improves the environment for others—I won't have any fun if my coworkers can't have fun with me.

Case Study: Casual Days

In an attempt to increase job satisfaction among employees, a few firms are experimenting with what they call casual or "dress down" days. More appropriate for some firms than others, the idea is to encourage employees to wear casual clothing one day each week. Most companies select Friday, but a few organizations prefer Monday, claiming that it sets the stage for a better week.

Two of the 10 sources of job satisfaction are affected by such an experiment. Wearing more casual clothing seems to facilitate more social interaction and relax the work environment.

A first analysis may show management that there is too much socializing, and productivity may be impaired or customers neglected. It might be, however, that the opposite is true.

Each organization must experiment and decide if job satisfaction was increased. If job satisfaction is increased, it is reasonable to assume that productivity will, in the long run, also increase.

Would you vote for a casual day where you work? Justify your position.

_____

_____

_____

Author's Response

Casual days make more sense for some organizations (or departments) than for others. Factors to consider include whether employees meet customers and, if so, what kinds of clients are served; image of organization; safety factors; whether employees have voted for such days; impact on productivity, quality control and personnel retention. Employees who are engaged in repetitive, task-oriented work out of customer sight may benefit the most.

Case Study: All or Nothing

Lin and Grover spent lunch comparing and discussing their *Job Satisfaction Profiles*. Lin's profile shows that she rated herself five or under in four categories. Grover's profile shows a low score in three.

Lin comments: ''You know, Grover, I'm not sure that I am prepared to commit myself to upgrading my scores, but if I decide to, I'm going to work on all 10. Here's why. I figure if I am already getting satisfaction from a few sources, my efforts will pay bigger dividends if I concentrate on getting more out of them instead of just working on those sources where I had low scores. I think it's a good idea not only to play your winners, but also bring up the sources of satisfaction you have ignored or neglected. If I do it at all I might as well commit myself to all 10 sources instead of just pulling up a few low scores.''

''Not me,'' replied Grover. ''I've already decided that I will focus on my three low sources and ignore those where I am already doing well. I believe the goal should be to gain a balance among all 10 sources—that is, be at a minimum above-average in all areas so you do not miss any of the satisfactions. I figure the only way I can pull myself up in my low categories is to concentrate on them. I never do well when I bite off more than I can chew.''

Do you agree with Lin or Grover? Explain your choice.

_____

_____

_____

Author's Response

It is tempting to support both approaches because everyone is different. Lin, working to improve all 10 sources, may find she gets more additional satisfaction than Grover because she will be more aware of all 10 sources. Grover seems more highly motivated to increase his score in his three chosen sources. Most people will succeed with Grover's approach because it is far better to increase low scores than to try to improve in too many areas at the same time and give up.

EMPOWER YOURSELF

As employees learn to tap the sources of job satisfaction, they discover that many different and surprising things happen to them. They complain less and enjoy their working hours more. They build better working relationships with fellow employees. They discover that they are appreciated more by management and doors of opportunity that were previously closed now open. But the biggest surprise of all is when employees realize that they have empowered themselves.

Why does gaining more job satisfaction give one more self-confidence, strength, prestige or feeling of importance? Study the two columns below for your answer. On the left are the sources of satisfaction. On the right are the results that empower you. Fill in the blanks and compare your answers with those at the bottom of the page.

Sources of Satisfaction	Psychological Results
1. *PRODUCTIVITY*	You place a higher _____ upon yourself.
2. *QUALITY OF WORK*	You have more _____ for your abilities.
3. *LEARNING*	You become more _____ .
4. *EXPRESSING CREATIVITY*	You _____ better.
5. *PROFESSIONALISM*	Your _____ improves.
6. *RECOGNITION*	Your _____ soars.
7. *TEAMWORK*	You demonstrate you can build stronger coworker _____ .
8. *SOCIAL SATISFACTION*	More coworkers will _____ you for leadership roles.
9. *PERSONAL GROWTH*	You gather _____ .
10. *WORK ENVIRONMENT REWARDS*	You will _____ your job more.

Missing words: 1. value **2.** respect **3.** competitive **4.** communicate **5.** image **6.** self-confidence **7.** relationships **8.** support **9.** momentum **10.** appreciate

P A R T

IV

Attitude Traps

WHICH TRAP ARE YOU CAUGHT IN?

Many employees who score low on the *Job Satisfaction Scale* may not be aware of the traps they must avoid before they achieve maximum satisfaction. These traps come in the form of attitudes and must be discarded before progress can be made.

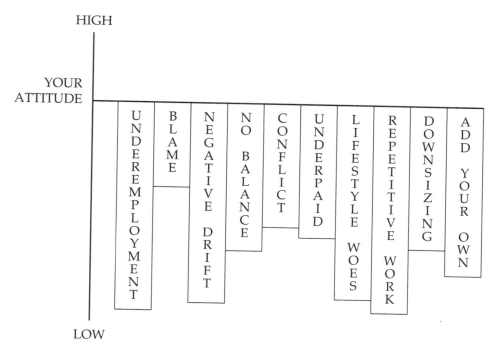

As you take your journey to greater job satisfaction, be aware of your attitude traps. Here are a few tips:

► If you admit to yourself that you are trapped, get out before you proceed.

► Although you may not be caught in one of the traps, recognize your vulnerability to falling in later.

► Maintaining job satisfaction on a long-term basis may require that you change your behavior. If so, face the problem and do something about it.

Attitude Trap #1: Singing the Underemployed Blues

Some experts claim that more than half of the workforce is underemployed. Here are some reasons why this could be true.

"By the time I get to use the skills I learned in college, they will be outmoded."

- Many individuals have trained for higher level jobs that are no longer available.

- Workers may become trapped in obsolete jobs because they don't retrain themselves or perhaps decide not to move to a new location where better jobs exist.

- One spouse sticks with a bad job so the other can hold one that isn't.

- Firms that have laid workers off have fewer challenging jobs.

What about you? Do you feel underemployed? If so, when you completed the *Job Satisfaction Scale* you might have said to yourself: "I'm not getting much job satisfaction because I'm stuck in a job that can't challenge me." This is a tough situation, but if you can't get your job to challenge you, then challenge yourself.

1. Change your mental focus and start making your job more than it is.

2. Initiate a Plan B—that is, prepare for a better job elsewhere.

3. Supplement your full-time job with a part-time job so that the combination of two jobs will challenge you.

You won't get much satisfaction from your job if you keep singing the underemployed blues.

CHECK ONE

☐ This trap is a problem of mine and keeps me from achieving the job satisfaction I seek.

☐ I am vulnerable to this trap. It may catch me later.

☐ This trap is not a problem now and I will not allow it to become one later.

Attitude Trap #2: Playing the Blame Game

Many employees, especially during periods of instability and change, scuttle their future because they blame the past for the situation in which they find themselves today.

"You lose in all directions when you blame your job for your problems."

"I chose the wrong career and now I'm stuck. If I had entered the labor market 10 years ago, I would be set by now."

"I quit my old job to go into real estate just before the downturn. Everything in life is just a matter of timing."

"If we could sell our home we would be able to move to a better labor market and things would improve."

"If my college counselor had gotten me on the right career track, I wouldn't be in this predicament."

Change always leaves a wake of people behind who refuse to adjust their attitudes. They allow circumstances to control their lives. Playing the blame game is the easy way out. Taking a new look at themselves, their jobs and adopting new attitudes is the tough way out.

Here are some options to consider.

1. Admit that playing the blame game is a sport designed for losers. Learn to play a different game.

2. Make plans for a career change or a business of your own if your job is obsolete.

3. Take a vacation and come back with a new attitude. Until you can focus on a positive future, little job satisfaction should be anticipated.

CHECK ONE

☐ This trap is a problem of mine and keeps me from achieving the job satisfaction I seek.

☐ I am vulnerable to this trap. It may catch me later.

☐ This trap is not a problem now and I will not allow it to become one later.

Attitude Trap #3: Succumbing to Negative Drift

Negative drift is a phenomenon that replaces your positive thoughts with negative ones. It is like a black cloud that covers your focus on life. Negative drift is always active—it keeps pushing the negative side of life to center stage. What are the causes?

If you don't develop a counterforce, negative drift will take over.

- Drugs, crime, violence, traffic and litigation are more prolific today than at any period in the past.
- Jobs are more stressful and competition for them is greater.
- The media provides an overdose of negative images.

A counterforce is needed, and for most people, an effective counterforce is a more positive attitude. Push negative drift back to the outer perimeter of your thinking by concentrating on the positive factors in your life. For example, let's assume that you feel increasingly negative about your job. Negative drift is taking over. What can you do? Perhaps you can take a mini vacation weekend and write out both the positive and negative factors of your present job. Then, when you return to work, force yourself to think and talk about only the positive factors. Keep this up for a few days and you will discover that you have a counterforce that may do the trick. Keep in mind that:

1. Attitude is the way you look at things. Any job has positive and negative factors. A worker with a positive attitude focuses primarily on the positive and tries to change or minimize the negative.

2. To control negative drift (you cannot eliminate it), use every technique in the book to stay positive. If you let your guard down, negative drift takes over.

3. When you seriously attempt to gain job satisfaction from one or all of the 10 sources, you are, in effect, maintaining a positive attitude and fighting off negative drift.

CHECK ONE

☐ This trap is a problem of mine and keeps me from achieving the job satisfaction I seek.

☐ I am vulnerable to this trap. It may catch me later.

☐ This trap is not a problem now and I will not allow it to become one later.

Attitude Trap #4: Failing to Balance Home and Career

Most people work not to gain job satisfaction, but to accommodate and improve their world away from work. Nothing is wrong with this. But when your lifestyle is so busy, demanding or out of control that you can't give your job the energy and attention it deserves, then your job and lifestyle need to be put back into a better balance.

"Job satisfaction is based upon a balance between work and your lifestyle. One should not be sacrificed for the other."

- Anyone with a family who holds down a challenging office job during the day and also works at night is probably out of balance.

- Anyone who is remodeling a home, holding down a weekend job to pay for it and has a demanding regular job might be out of balance.

- Anyone raising a family alone who tries to give the children everything two-parent families give their children could be out of balance, especially if the individual holds a demanding job and works a lot of overtime.

Everyone needs to work out the best balance possible so that neither lifestyle or job is neglected. Burning a candle at both ends is fun as long as the ends are far enough apart to prevent burnout in the middle, but it takes organization and planning beyond normal demands. Here are a few tips:

1. If you are married, work out a plan for balancing with your spouse. Keep your long-term goals in sight and the pressure even. This will take continuous communication.

2. If you are single with family demands, let a friend help you balance things out. Keep in mind that you need some time for yourself.

3. For most people, neglecting jobs to satisfy lifestyle demands is a mistake. Lifestyles are built on jobs more than the other way around.

CHECK ONE

☐ This trap is a problem of mine and keeps me from achieving the job satisfaction I seek.

☐ I am vulnerable to this trap. It may catch me later.

☐ This trap is not a problem now and I will not allow it to become one later.

Attitude Trap #5: Conflicts with Your Boss

If your supervisor is living up to your expectations of what a great boss should be, this page is a waste of your time. If not, it could be the most important page in the book.

"It's not easy being a boss these days."

The wrong supervisor can accelerate negative drift faster than any other job factor. For years researchers have reported that more than 50 percent of voluntary resignations come from a supervisory/employee conflict. Most employees have had to adjust at some time to a difficult, demanding and perhaps unfair boss. Bosses, like the rest of us, are not perfect.

Assume you have a difficult supervisor. You frequently become frustrated carrying out your duties. The conflict between you may not be major, but it does exist. What can you do about it?

Take a candid look at the relationship between you and your boss. Try to forget the personality at the other end. Visualize a relationship line that both you and your boss might keep free of conflicts. Recognize that this can be accomplished regardless of the personalities involved. How do you do this? First, remember that the life blood of any relationship is frequent communication. Second, acknowledge that your boss expects things from you (productivity, quality performance, etc.) and you want certain rewards in return (recognition, opportunity to learn, salary increases, etc.). When these rewards are somewhat in balance, a healthy relationship usually exists. Here are some additional tips:

1. Take a more positive look at the relationship line between you and your boss. Start from scratch. Give your boss a few breaks when it comes to management style. You may not be perfect, either.

2. Do your part by doing your job well.

3. Refuse to be victimized. Keep in mind that your positive attitude is your most priceless possession and it belongs to you. Your boss does not own it.

4. If you try but can't improve the relationship, find another job or obtain a transfer.

CHECK ONE

☐ This trap is a problem of mine and keeps me from achieving the job satisfaction I seek.

☐ I am vulnerable to this trap. It may catch me later.

☐ This trap is not a problem now and I will not allow it to become one later.

Attitude Trap #6: Falling for the Underpaid Melody

It is good to put a high value on your services. This is what professionals do. But once you have accepted a salary and benefit package, it is self-defeating to allow it to nudge you into a negative attitude. Here's why.

"Workers who always complain about their pay, seldom focus on the good side of their jobs and, as a result, their attitudes suffer so they get little job satisfaction.

- When you tell yourself that you are worth more than you are paid, you diminish yourself. You are saying that you are being treated as a second-class worker. You allow your negative attitude to trap you at the bottom of the pile instead of push you up the ladder where you will be paid more.

- When you hear that someone makes more money than you do, you might think that your job is more demanding and that he or she is just lucky. Don't let negative drift take over and turn you into a victim.

- Comparing salaries is most difficult, because it is almost impossible to do a legitimate analysis without a responsible matrix.

What can you do to offset these possibilities?

1. Think job satisfaction first, remuneration second.

2. Put yourself in a position where you will be offered a higher paying role or upgrade your skills so that you will be wanted elsewhere.

3. Protect your positive attitude by discounting some of the highly paid jobs you hear about.

4. Increase your income, if necessary, through a second job that won't upset your lifestyle balance.

5. If you still remain convinced that you are unfairly underpaid, start a Plan B and find a job where your value will be recognized.

CHECK ONE

☐ This trap is a problem of mine and keeps me from achieving the job satisfaction I seek.

☐ I am vulnerable to this trap. It may catch me later.

☐ This trap is not a problem now and I will not allow it to become one later.

Achieving Job Satisfaction

Attitude Trap #7: Reaching Job Lows Because of Lifestyle Woes

Some employees let their lifestyles interfere with their job satisfaction and then blame their jobs for the mess they are in. These people bring their problems to work with them, complain a lot and permit their concentration to drift away from their work. Their griping also distracts coworkers.

"If you can't get your act together at home, you'll have trouble getting it together at work."

Shannon and her husband are in such a hurry to reach a more comfortable standard of living that she works full-time, and Ken, her husband, holds down one full- and one part-time job. As they go about achieving this goal, they drive new cars, keep their children in private schools, take expensive vacations and live in a more luxurious home than they need or can afford. The pressure to upgrade their lifestyle results in less and less job satisfaction and, as a result, their career progress begins to suffer.

When you permit lifestyle problems to affect work attitudes until you are blinded to the sources of job satisfaction, the trap is sprung and the damage is severe. What can you do? Here are some principles to help guide you.

1. The balance between home and career is more delicate and difficult to maintain than most employees think. It requires constant attention.

2. Balancing is a two-way street. High job satisfaction spills over and enhances one's lifestyle. Low job satisfaction ruins it.

3. Blaming poor job performance on off-job problems is not fair to your job, your employer, your family or yourself.

CHECK ONE

☐ This trap is a problem of mine and keeps me from achieving the job satisfaction I seek.

☐ I am vulnerable to this trap. It may catch me later.

☐ This trap is not a problem now and I will not allow it to become one later.

Attitude Trap #8: Doing the Same Old Thing Over and Over

The more repetitive a job becomes, the more difficult it is to gain job satisfaction. Routine work opens the door to negative drift. Soon the employee just tries to get through the day without giving any thought to job satisfaction.

The problem in having a repetitive job is keeping your concentration high so that you don't allow quality standards to slip.

Of course, some employees learn to like their routine jobs because they can save their energy for leisure pursuits, the pressures are less and they can save themselves for moonlighting opportunities.

Most employees, however, continue to strive for job satisfaction even though their jobs demand periods where they use certain skills over and over.

What can these workers do to keep their productivity and quality standards high? What can they do to stay professional?

1. Exploit some sources over others. For example, during breaks and lunch periods, socialize with coworkers, have some fun and try to get physical exercise.

2. Have a learning goal. Use your spare time to learn new skills that you apply to other parts of a business.

3. Make it known that you would like to move into a more challenging position.

4. Do whatever it takes to stay positive, but if you find yourself falling deeper and deeper into a negative trap, get serious about a plan B and make a career change.

CHECK ONE

☐ This trap is a problem of mine and keeps me from achieving the job satisfaction I seek.

☐ I am vulnerable to this trap. It may catch me later.

☐ This trap is not a problem now and I will see to it that it won't become one later.

Achieving Job Satisfaction

Attitude Trap #9: Coping with the Big Freeze Lullaby

Factory closures and corporate layoffs have a huge negative effect on morale. Workers who remain, instead of feeling grateful and appreciative, usually feel depressed. Why?

"It is not easy to get your attitude up once your organization has gone through downsizing. Things never seem to get back to where they were."

- Morale plummets because you don't know what will happen next. Sometimes there is guilt because friends didn't survive the layoff.

- You find yourself doing two jobs instead of one.

- Work loads are poorly distributed. Some departments are overloaded; others are left with less to do.

- Layoffs introduce other cutbacks: hiring freezes, wage freezes, and elimination of cost-of-living adjustments.

Employees left behind often need to make twice the effort to protect and maintain job satisfaction, let alone increase it.

1. After layoffs, improving job satisfaction is more important than ever—to you and to your firm.

2. Face the new reality of your situation without looking back to the way things were.

3. Hold on to your long-term goals.

4. Remember that opportunities surface during any rebuilding process.

CHECK ONE

☐ This trap is a problem of mine and keeps me from achieving the job satisfaction I seek.

☐ I am vulnerable to this trap. It may catch me later.

☐ This trap is not a problem now and I will see to it that it won't become one later.

OTHER TRAPS

Although these attitude traps may be the major barriers to overcome, the list is incomplete. Here are a few additional traps that can keep you from finding job satisfaction:

- Failure to build friendly relationships with coworkers can mean isolation and lost social contacts and on-the-job fun.

- Some employees who accept jobs knowing that they are underemployed often project a superior attitude and thereby restrict the satisfaction they receive from their jobs. Others who feel inferior to their fellow employees withdraw from opportunities to communicate on a friendly basis and become vulnerable to misunderstandings.

- It is estimated that one out of 10 workers has a drug dependency of some kind. Alcohol is the prime suspect. Such a dependency can keep an employee from finding and enjoying job satisfaction.

- Coworkers who have fallen into an attitude trap can pull you down with them.

- Add your own traps:

    1. _____

    2. _____

    3. _____

P A R T

V

Exercises to Close the Gap

EXERCISE #1: WORKSHOP GUIDE

This workshop guide is designed to assist supervisors who want to increase the job satisfaction of their employees through group meetings. This part is divided into two programs. Program 1 is for those departments that provide a copy of this book to each employee. Program 2 is for those supervisors who provide only the ''Job Satisfaction Scale'' to each employee, but keep a copy of the book available on a loan basis.

Program 1: With a Book for Each Participant

First One-Hour Session

The steps that follow are recommended when two one-hour sessions are scheduled on different days in two successive weeks. When more or less time is available, each step can be expanded or shortened to meet the time schedule. Obviously, the more time available the more discussion is possible.

STEP 1: Pass out the book and describe it. Say that because on-the-job discussion time is limited, the book is provided for employees to take home for further study.

STEP 2: Take five minutes to introduce Part I, ''Accepting the Challenge.''

STEP 3: Have employees complete the ''Job Satisfaction Scale'' in Part II.

STEP 4: Explain in advance that each scale will be picked up for a short time to compile average scores for all employees. Stress that employees need not sign their names, but some identifying mark is necessary, since the scales will be returned. Pick up the books so that a designated employee can compile the scores.

STEP 5: While the average score for each source is being determined, discuss Part III. Ask, ''Do you agree with the 10 sources of job satisfaction?''

STEP 6: Read the average scores for each of the 10 sources of job satisfaction.

STEP 7: Discuss the results.

STEP 8: Return the books so employees can do further reading on their own time. Tell them to bring the books with them for the next meeting.

These steps are suggestions only. Each supervisor must adapt them for each situation and time limitations.

EXERCISE #1: WORKSHOP GUIDE (continued)

If only one hour is available, the supervisor might offer to check back on individuals to evaluate what job satisfaction improvements might have been made.

Second One-Hour Session

STEP 9: Start the second hour by asking for reactions to the first session and the book.

STEP 10: Discuss "Attitude Traps."

STEP 11: Ask employees to make suggestions on how you, as their supervisor, can help them find more job satisfaction.

STEP 12: Through a show of hands, discover how many employees would like to take the scale a second time in 60 days so that scores can be compared.

Program 2: With Job Satisfaction Scale Only

First One-Hour Session

The steps that follow are recommended when two one-hour sessions are scheduled on different days in two successive weeks. When more or less time is available, each step can be expanded or shortened to meet the time schedule. Obviously, the more time available the more discussion is possible.

STEP 1: Hold up a copy of the book *Achieving Job Satisfaction.* Say that you have only one (or two) copies and that it will be made available on a rotating basis to departmental employees.

STEP 2: Discuss the challenge of the book (first seven pages). You might wish to read one or two of the pages aloud.

STEP 3: Pass out a copy of the Job Satisfaction Scale to each participant. Read the introduction.

STEP 4: Have each employee complete the scale. Explain in advance that each scale will be picked up for a short time to compile average scores for all employees. Stress that employees need not sign their names, but some identifying mark is necessary, since scales will be returned.

STEP 5: While a designated employee is compiling the average score for each source, ask for reactions. For example, ask, "How many of you agree that the sources in the exercise are the primary psychological ones?"

STEP 6: Read the average scores for each of the 10 sources of job satisfaction.

STEP 7: Discuss the results.

STEP 8: Return the Job Satisfaction Scales and suggest that coworkers compare scores.

These steps are suggestions only. Each supervisor must adapt them for each situation and time limitations.

If only one hour is available (no second meeting), the supervisor might offer to check back with each individual to evaluate the value of completing and discussing the job satisfaction sources.

EXERCISE #1: WORKSHOP GUIDE (continued)

Second One-Hour Session

STEP 9: Start the second hour by asking for reactions to the first session. Has anyone made an extra effort to increase job satisfaction?

STEP 10: Discuss Part IV, "Attitude Traps." If possible, list them on a board or sheet of paper.

STEP 11: Ask employees to make suggestions on how you, as their supervisor, can help them find more job satisfaction.

STEP 12: Through a show of hands, discover how many employees would like to take the scale a second time in 60 days so that scores can be compared.

NOTE TO SUPERVISORS

Field testing indicates that many departments hold short meetings (perhaps 20 minutes) each week. It is possible to administer the *Job Satisfaction Scale* in the time allotted without scheduling longer meetings. Once you have read and analyzed the book, you can adapt the material to your own needs.

In some cases, especially with larger organizations, the training department may conduct seminars for both supervisors and employees.

EXERCISE #2: JOB SATISFACTION ASSESSMENT

Once supervisors have administered the *Job Satisfaction Scale* to their employees, they are in a position to compare results with the norms (see pages 23 & 27) to determine what action to take. At this point, supervisors might decide to build up the weak sources and neglect those already high. A better policy, however, is to take all possible steps to see that employees increase their job satisfaction in *all categories*.

Listed on the following pages are suggestions for increasing job satisfaction and action steps that can be taken to improve employee's job satisfaction from each of the ten sources. Keep in mind that the easier you make it to find job satisfaction, the more you *will* find it.

Directions for Supervisors:

If you are a supervisor, review each source and accompanying suggestions for improvements. Place a plus ''+'' by each item that you use currently and a minus ''−'' by those items you have not used.

Directions for Employees:

If you are an employee, review each source and accompanying suggestions for improvements. Place a plus ''+'' by each suggestion that your supervisor is using currently and a minus ''−'' by those items that have not been used.

1. *PRODUCTIVITY*

Supervisors who know how to establish goals and motivate their people to reach them enhance the job satisfaction employees receive. Three sound guides to follow are:

''I may be an old-fashioned boss but I still find weekly and monthly productivity goals effective.''

——— Establish reachable goals that are not counter-productive to employee attitudes.

——— Provide frequent reports on the progress being made. Share both the ups and downs of productivity data.

——— Provide compliments and rewards when increases occur—discuss causes when figures drop.

EXERCISE #2: JOB SATISFACTION ASSESSMENT (continued)

2. *QUALITY OF WORK*

Although some employees will gain more satisfaction out of exceeding quality standards than others, quality work should be as important a goal as quantity. Consider these rules:

"Setting productivity goals without quality standards is a farce."

_____ Compliment employees as freely on quality work as on reaching quantity goals.

_____ Share all significant complaints received from clients or customers. Discuss how corrections can be made.

_____ Consider giving out quality buttons, plaques, or other rewards to those who reach quality standards. Vary rewards so they do not become routine and ineffective.

3. *LEARNING*

Most employees recognize that the more they can learn from one job the more it will help them in other jobs down the road. Supervisors should encourage this kind of thinking so that their employees will gain more satisfaction from accepting and completing difficult assignments. Here are three tips that might help:

"I was a supervisor three years before I realized I was also a teacher."

_____ Ask each employee to turn in their learning goals so you can assist in reaching them.

_____ Make a practice of rotating assignments among team members so that learning becomes a daily challenge.

_____ Whenever possible, provide learning materials.

4. *EXPRESSING CREATIVITY*

Employees gain satisfaction when they submit an idea that is accepted or when they turn in an assignment that goes beyond what would normally be expected. They also express creativity in the way they communicate and dress. The more creative employees are encouraged to be, the more satisfaction they will feel. Consider these techniques:

_____ Discover the hidden talents of your staff (artistic, musical, cooking, etc.) and seek ways to let them express their talents on the job; for example, during birthday, transfer and retirement parties.

_____ Consider talents when making work assignments.

_____ Consider giving creativity awards to those who create something worthy of special attention.

"I have yet to discover an employee who is void of some creative talent."

5. *PROFESSIONALISM*

Employees with the same ability will not necessarily have the same level of professionalism. Are the professionals reinforcing their egos? Does it give them more self-esteem? Or is it because their jobs simply mean more to them?

Whatever it is, professionals perform their work with more care and accuracy than do others. As a result, they gain more job satisfaction. How can you encourage more professionalism among your staff? Consider these suggestions:

_____ Set a better example yourself.

_____ Discuss professionalism and job ethics as they apply to your career area.

_____ Compliment those who dress and conduct themselves in a way to encourage more professionalism among coworkers.

"Have you noticed that employees who take pride in their work also take pride in their appearance?"

EXERCISE #: JOB SATISFACTION ASSESSEMNT (continued)

6. *RECOGNITION*

"Some of my fellow super-visors are so stingy in handing out compliments you would think each one had a $100 bill attached to it."

Many employees need a constant stream of rewards to perform at high levels. Even those who do well with fewer compliments appreciate them when they are deserved and sincere. Why then are many supervisors so miserly in delivering them? Perhaps they fear that being generous will make them less valuable. Perhaps they think that by paying compliments they will lose some of their authority or leadership. The source of satisfaction that normally receives the lowest score is failure to receive enough recognition. How might you correct this? Here are some possibilities:

_____ Form the practice of seeking behavioral patterns among employees who deserve a sincere compliment. Then give it!

_____ Acknowledge that recognition comes in many forms—a special assignment, personal time off, receiving a trophy, etc. Also recognize that nothing will replace a personal, verbal compliment that takes only a moment to deliver.

_____ Now that you know how your employees feel about recognition (see your summary of employee *Job Satisfaction Scales*) take a second survey in a few months to discover how effective the above actions might be for you.

7. *SOCIALIZING*

More socializing takes place under the team concept than the traditional pyramid form of authority. Successful team leaders claim the time devoted to socialization is a small price to pay for the additional productivity that usually comes from the team environment. Each supervisor, of course, must decide how much socializing should take place and when it is appropriate. For many employees, spending some time with coworkers (breaks, lunch and inactive periods) is a major source of job satisfaction. What can the supervisor do to enhance this reward? Try these suggestions:

"Socializing on the job is great as long as productivity and customers are not neglected."

_____ Strike the right balance between quality production and a few periods of social relaxation, but let your staff know that socializing is not the same as long personal telephone calls.

_____ Should you feel that socializing is getting out of hand, try to handle it without embarrassing your staff by breaking up a social gathering. Rather, try to handle it quietly on the side on an individual basis. One technique is to join in with a social group for a few moments and then assign one or two tasks so that everyone understands that their jobs are waiting. Every working team requires leadership, and most employees want you to establish a fair and consistent approach.

EXERCISE #: JOB SATISFACTION ASSESSMENT (continued)

8. TEAMWORK

"I am convinced that the main reason team members produce more is because the team approach eventually leads to greater job satisfaction for all members."

Successful teams do get certain psychological rewards, which are the result of the dynamics of interplay that occur as people work together to achieve a common goal. How might you move more in the direction of a true team operation in your department so that your people will receive more team rewards? Consider these moves:

_____ Involve your people more in the decision-making process so that they can share more in the responsibility of the operation.

_____ Communicate more—both upward and downward.

_____ Empower your employees to the point that they manage themselves more.

9. PERSONAL GROWTH

"I get great pleasure from helping a worthy employee outgrow the jobs in my small business and move on."

In most organizations, an employee's personal growth is measured by the supervisor during the annual formal appraisal process. When employees show measurable progress over the previous report, they often express their feelings of satisfaction and immediately set new goals for themselves. How can you accelerate the growth patterns of your employees? Here are some suggestions:

_____ Look for special growth opportunities for your employees. Examples: attending a seminar or convention, counseling another employee, doing a special written report or attending a meeting with you.

_____ Accept the philosophy that preparing an employee for a better company job outside of your department is the best contribution you can make to your firm. Share this philosophy with all your team members.

_____ Instill the "mutual reward" theory in the minds of your staff. Make sure they fully understand that the best way to build lasting working relationships is to function in such a way that both parties win. Adopt this policy yourself.

10. WORK ENVIRONMENT

"It did wonders for my self-esteem when we moved to a new head-quarters build-ing and I had a new office of my own with carpeting and an outside window."

Management plays a major role in helping employees gain satisfaction from their work environment. No matter where you work, clean restrooms, a nice place to eat lunch and other physical conditions are important. As a supervisor, however, you have the responsibility of making the most of the environment upper management has assigned you. What might you do to improve what you have been given? Here are a few suggestions:

_____ Give special treatment to those custodial people assigned to keep your department clean.

_____ Listen carefully and follow through on any complaints from your staff. New lighting, repainting, fixing an air conditioner or getting new equipment is part of your job.

_____ Encourage your staff to bring fresh flowers, family pictures, etc. Give employees as much freedom as possible to decorate their work stations.

Follow-up for Supervisors:

Now review the total number of pluses and minuses. If there are a significant number of minuses, this would be a good time to develop a plan of action to begin to incorporate suggestions for improving your employees' job satisfaction.

Follow-up for Employees:

At the end of this exercise, schedule time with your supervisor to review each item that you marked with a minus and develop an action plan that will help you get more job satisfaction.

Remember: Ultimately, it is up to each individual to be responsible for his or her own job satisfaction.

EXERCISE #3: 15 QUESTIONS

In this exercise, please assume you are a participant in a seminar on *Job Satisfaction* and your instructor is welcoming questions. Read each of the questions and pick the five that are the most important to you. Answer these five, in the spaces provided, as you think the instructor would answer them. When you are finished, turn to pages 81–85 for the authors suggested responses.

1. Are the expectations of higher job satisfaction, as encouraged in this book, realistic?

_____

_____

_____

_____

2. Do most workers really try to get satisfaction from their jobs?

_____

_____

_____

_____

3. Why is it that most workers do not know the sources of job satisfaction?

_____

_____

_____

_____

4. Do employees who perform with minimum productivity miss out on a major source of job satisfaction?

_____

_____

_____

_____

5. Are some workers motivated to keep their productivity above average, but still recognize that they are not living up to their potential?

_____

_____

_____

_____

6. What percentage of workers would you estimate have stopped learning on their jobs?

_____

_____

_____

_____

7. Are the 10 sources of job satisfaction found in the _Job Satisfaction Scale_ the only sources?

_____

_____

_____

_____

EXERCISE #3: 15 QUESTIONS (continued)

8. Do most workers needlessly allow their jobs to beat them down?

_____

_____

_____

_____

9. When individuals are in the middle of a severe job depression, can they pull themselves back up without making a job or career change?

_____

_____

_____

_____

10. Is getting more job satisfaction from the sources really a matter of attitude?

_____

_____

_____

_____

11. At what point should one accept the inevitability of a career change to gain greater satisfaction?

_____

_____

_____

_____

12. How can management expect employees to gain high job satisfaction when they don't provide all of the incentives at their disposal?

_____

_____

_____

_____

13. Once achieved, how can one hold on to higher job satisfaction?

_____

_____

_____

_____

14. Is it true that supervisors or managers who complete the _Job Satisfaction Scale_ themselves will be more helpful in assisting their employees to gain more satisfaction from their jobs?

_____

_____

_____

_____

15. Does greater job satisfaction really increase productivity?

_____

_____

_____

_____

A SELF-IMPROVEMENT PLAN

Individuals who want to increase the personal satisfaction they received from their jobs can, of course, devise a system of their own.

Some highly disciplined, highly motivated employees can make behavioral changes more easily than others. Psychologists have trouble explaining just why this is the case. All we know is that these exceptional people seem to make binding contracts with themselves and then stick with them. Most of us need additional assistance.

Case Study: Rick and Rose

Rick and Rose are opposites in this respect.

Rick is uncertain about whether he should make a change in the first place, but if he makes a commitment, he carries it out. Is it because he is highly organized? Is Rick more goal-oriented than others? For example, if you were to present an idea to Rick that would provide him with more job satisfaction and he recognized it as valid, he would devise a system that would incorporate the change into his behavioral patterns. He would reject a system proposed by others in favor of his own.

Rose, on the other hand, keeps signing up for self-improvement programs (especially those connected with weight reduction), but seldom does she finish a course. She wants to improve her life and would love to get more satisfaction from her job, but she probably won't do anything about it. Why can't Rose make a commitment and follow through like Rick? It is because she is a procrastinator and can't bridge the gap between wanting to change and doing it? Does Rose need a traumatic event to shock her into making behavioral changes that will improve her life? Or does she need a step-by-step system devised by someone else?

Review

Are you more like Rick or more like Rose? _____

Explain _____

_____

Many of us are more like Rose than Rick. We would appreciate and often need a simple system that will help us incorporate a change we really want into our behavioral patterns. Consider the five-day attitude improvement plan that follows.

THE FIVE-DAY PLAN

This simple, progressive system can start providing additional job satisfaction immediately. The five-day plan invites you to concentrate one day at a time on each of your five lowest scores in a prescribed manner. Here are the rules.

1. Select the five sources from which you desire to gain more satisfaction.

2. Write these sources (personal productivity, recognition, team rewards, etc.) on a small card or piece of paper that will fit into your billfold.

3. Memorize them.

4. Review the card each day for a full week and choose one source to concentrate on per day. For example, you might have been neglecting relationships with coworkers and, as a result, you do not enjoy your breaks as much as you did. Solution? Do little things to repair relationships—be more friendly or pay some deserved compliments.

5. Stay with this option until you have refocused your attitude on the five sources of satisfaction you selected in the first place.

You may decide that there are more or less than five sources upon which you wish to concentrate. In that case, simply extend or reduce the days to fit the sources from which you wish to gain greater satisfaction. You could, for example, concentrate on seven sources or even all 10; or, you might want to improve the satisfaction you gain from only three or four sources. As long as you commit yourself to concentrate one day on each source, the system will provide results. Once you have discovered that it can be reinforcing to gain more satisfaction from a single source, you may wish to work on one or more you did not include on your original list.

No matter how many sources of satisfaction you decide to improve, be sure to give yourself a reward when you have completed this plan. This reward, plus the new job satisfaction you receive, will help you view your job in a more positive way.

ANTICIPATE THESE RESULTS

If you conscientiously apply the option of your choice you can anticipate these results:

► You will become more positive in the way you look at your specific job and work in general.

► You will discover sources of job satisfaction that you did not previously know existed.

► Chances are good that you will realize you have underestimated the potential of your present job.

► Relationships with your supervisor and coworkers will improve.

► You will be successful in eliminating some of the traps or barriers that have prevented you from reaching higher levels of job satisfaction.

► Your sense of humor will improve.

► Your career opportunities will improve.

ANSWERS

The following are the author's suggested responses to the 15 Questions exercise on pages 74–77.

1. Yes, if the reader accepts the expectation theory, which states that the more you expect the more you are apt to get. Someone who is in touch with the sources of job satisfaction and expects to get more job satisfaction from them will do so. The trouble with most workers is that they have permitted themselves to become so bored and discouraged with their jobs that they no longer expect much. Their wishes are fulfilled; they receive what they expect to receive. The purpose of the *Job Satisfaction Scale* is to identify and raise expectations in 10 specific areas. Only those who raise their sights and expect more satisfaction from the sources will accomplish their goals.

2. No. Most workers let their tasks pull them down and give up as far as finding satisfaction is concerned. Many do not realize that finding satisfaction starts within, not from management. You can compare two workers in almost any job and sense the difference. For example, one flight attendant can view an airline job as an adventure where customers are enjoyable and satisfaction is gained from serving them better—thus almost all sources of job satisfaction are tapped. Another flight attendant may view the job as something to get through without any attempt to gain personal satisfaction. It is a matter of attitude or focus. Those who make the effort to draw satisfaction from all the sources will enjoy their work more and do it better. They come out ahead and so do their employers.

3. Most workers have been trained to view work as a four-letter word. Work is work and you get it over with so you can find satisfaction in your after-work hours. Some of this attitude goes back to the days when many men spent their working hours in a coal or copper mine, where they were lucky to survive. To convert people who have been taught to dread work to seek the satisfactions in work is no easy task. When workers study the sources of job satisfaction, however, they slowly accept them, and then their minds open up. Little has been done to help people understand the psychology of work. Too often it has been drowned out by management-worker conflicts.

ANSWERS (continued)

4. Yes. These individuals seem to think that the less work they do, the happier they will be. They reject the idea that inactivity on a job turns their attitudes negative. Not only do they find less happiness on the job, they find less happiness in their personal lives. Just getting by is counter-productive because it is only when people try to live up to their potential that they achieve job satisfaction.

5. Yes. These highly capable employees often find it easy to maintain productivity levels above their coworkers' but they slow down after reaching such levels because they do not want to set a higher pace and become unpopular. Some of these employees do not seek management roles, so they figure that an above-average productivity level secures their jobs and any further activity would be useless.

6. A rough estimate would be more than 50 percent. If you accept the premise that every job has learning opportunities, the estimate could run higher. Again, it is a matter of attitude. Many employees who have stopped learning refuse to see that they do, in fact, have learning opportunities.

7. No. They do, however, represent the primary sources of job satisfaction. Field testing indicates that other sources of satisfaction usually fall into one of the 10 categories. Furthermore, psychological sources are often equally or more important to most individuals than physical sources of satisfaction such as rates of pay, benefits, company cafeterias or parking facilities.

8. Yes. There are, however, good reasons why this happens. One reason is just the routine of some jobs. Workers anticipate draggy days and their expectations are fulfilled. Some workers feel trapped by their jobs. They do not see any future and, as a result, they do not establish any stimulating goals. Negative drift takes.

Some workers get into conflicts with supervisors and coworkers, and having to live close to these strained relationships is uncomfortable and negative.

All of these situations can be offset. With effort, a worker can dissipate the routine, break insurmountable barriers and repair broken relationships with creativity.

It is easy to see why some jobs beat people down, but it need not happen if workers constantly seek job satisfaction and refuse to become negative.

9. In most cases, yes. To do this, however, they must usually step back from their jobs and force themselves to take a fresh look. They must start from scratch and find a higher degree of job satisfaction from each possible source. It can be a long journey back, but it can be done. Often workers in this situation need to receive an outside boost. For example, falling in love and getting married can cause workers to take a second, more positive look at their jobs.

A few people, even those with what should be satisfying jobs, always think that things will be greener with another firm, so they do not find the satisfaction available in their present jobs. These individuals always seem to feel they are in the wrong job or career—that their problem is not how they view their jobs (their attitudes), but the job itself.

ANSWERS (continued)

10. Yes, and for this reason. One must concentrate on each source and try to get satisfaction. Without this effort, nothing happens. For example, if you think you can get more satisfaction from higher productivity, you probably will. If you try to get more fun out a job, you probably will. However, it all starts with an attitude adjustment. You must want it to happen. How much additional satisfaction you gain is something else. The truth is that most people have become so dissatisfied with their jobs that they are negative about the possibilities of a turnaround. Until they perceive the opportunities and do something about it, they will make little improvement.

11. After one has made every possible effort to create more job satisfaction for one year, it is time to explore a new job in a new environment or prepare for a new career. This should be accomplished while the individual is still working. Sometimes just taking the step to make a job or career change is enough to motivate someone to seek more satisfaction in his or her present job and, without knowing it, the individual is propelled to change. On the other hand, one should not anticipate that simply making a job or career change will automatically create new job satisfaction. It may be an excellent opportunity, but gaining more satisfaction will still take effort.

12. It is true that it is easier to get greater job satisfaction from some managers than others. Some managers are better at giving recognition, some are in a position to set up better work environments, some allow more fun on the job and reward creative efforts where others do not. But surveys show that job satisfaction is not always higher in those organizations with the best personnel reputations. Of course, it is a win-win situation when management makes a supreme effort to provide job satisfaction and employees do the same. The problem comes even in the best of organizations when employees do not accept the responsibility of finding and creating their own satisfactions. In other words, employee attitude is the key. Management should do all that is possible and profitable to create a work environment where job satisfaction is easy to reach, but the effort must still come from the employees themselves. Management cannot force employees to seek job satisfaction. Attitude is a very private matter. No organization or supervisor owns the attitude of an employee.

13. Once individuals receive the rewards of greater job satisfaction, they will form habits that will prolong their achievements. Some of this will come about automatically. It is recommended, however, that all individuals check periodically on whether any progress is sustained. Such a check should include a review of the job satisfaction sources so that those neglected can be restored. It might also be worthwhile to do a second scale so you can compare improvements and discover where more effort should be made.

14. It is a reasonable assumption, because in going through the process themselves supervisors will gain additional insights and become believers. They will see that the best route to greater productivity is through an increase in job satisfaction. It should also convince a few that the team approach provides more job satisfaction.

15. Without establishing control groups and doing long-term experimentation, there will be no documentation that higher productivity follows greater job satisfaction. Yet, simple observation shows this to be a reasonable assumption. Employees who increase their job satisfaction appear to become more motivated, involved and professional in their approach to work.

NOTES

FOR OTHER FIFTY-MINUTE SELF-STUDY BOOKS
SEE THE BACK OF THIS BOOK.

We hope you enjoyed this book. If so, we have good news for you. This title is part of the best-selling *FIFTY-MINUTE*™ *Series* of books. All *Series* books are similar in size and identical in price. Several are supported with training videos (identified by the symbol ⓥ next to the title).

FIFTY-MINUTE Books and Videos are available from your distributor. A free catalog is available upon request from Crisp Publications, Inc., 1200 Hamilton Court, Menlo Park, California 94025.

FIFTY-MINUTE Series Books & Videos organized by general subject area.

Management Training:

ⓥ	Coaching & Counseling	68-8
	Conducting Training Sessions	193-7
	Delegating for Results	008-6
	Developing Instructional Design	076-0
ⓥ	Effective Meeting Skills	33-5
ⓥ	Empowerment	096-5
	Ethics in Business	69-6
	Goals & Goal Setting	183-X
	Handling the Difficult Employee	179-1
ⓥ	An Honest Day's Work: Motivating Employees	39-4
ⓥ	Increasing Employee Productivity	10-8
ⓥ	Leadership Skills for Women	62-9
	Learning to Lead	43-4
ⓥ	Managing Disagreement Constructively	41-6
ⓥ	Managing for Commitment	099-X
	Managing the Older Work Force	182-1
ⓥ	Managing Organizational Change	80-7
	Managing the Technical Employee	177-5
	Mentoring	123-6
ⓥ	The New Supervisor—Revised	120-1
	Personal Performance Contracts—Revised	12-2
ⓥ	Project Management	75-0
ⓥ	Quality at Work: A Personal Guide to Professional Standards	72-6
	Rate Your Skills As a Manager	101-5
	Recruiting Volunteers: A Guide for Nonprofits	141-4
	Risk Taking	076-9
	Selecting & Working with Consultants	87-4
	Self-Managing Teams	00-0
	Successful Negotiation—Revised	09-2
	Systematic Problem Solving & Decision Making	63-7

Human Resources & Wellness (continued):

Communications & Creativity:

Customer Service/Sales Training: